SCOTTISH MELODIES FOR TWO CELLOS

BY ANNE WITT

MB22232

Scottish Melodies for Two Cellos

The twenty-four pieces in this collection date from eighteenth and early nineteenth century Scotland. They include traditional airs and dance tunes originally for voice or fiddle. These arrangements are perfect for student and teacher, as well as cello colleagues.

The airs are enhanced by the cello's rich timbre. Some tunes make use of bagpipe drone effects. Some use the Scottish snap -- a short-long bowing -- which should be very snappy. The music is presented in sets of two or three tunes since most of the pieces are short. In a performance there should be no stop between the pieces, or at most, a brief pause. It would be quite appropriate to play through a tune two or three times before the segue to the next tune. It's up to the performer. You can also make up your own sets.

The traditional music of Scotland has unique and beautiful qualities. This new setting for two cellos will, I hope, expand the appreciation of this music.

Anne Witt

Thanks to Mary Ann Wallace, cellist, for playing through the music.

About the Author

Anne Witt began playing the viola as a child, always preferring its distinctly mellow tone. She studied art and music at Goucher College and has played in orchestras, chamber ensembles and string quartets over many years. She took up the bagpipe as an adult and performs regularly as a soloist at ceremonial events near her home. An interest in Scottish fiddle music prompted her to begin arranging fiddle tunes for viola. This book is also available in a version for two violas and two violins.

Contents

The Misty Dell

(Coire-Cheathaich)

Arranged by Anne Witt

This is an old Gaelic air.

16
mp
solo
20
mf
24
f
28
mf
1st turn page
segue
segue

Mairi's Wedding

The Devil's away with the Exciseman

Lively ♩ = 108

Arranged by Anne Witt

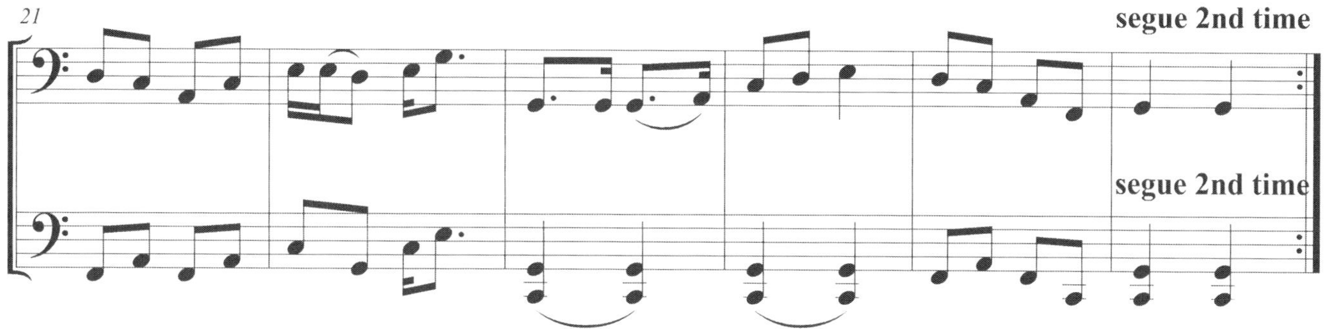

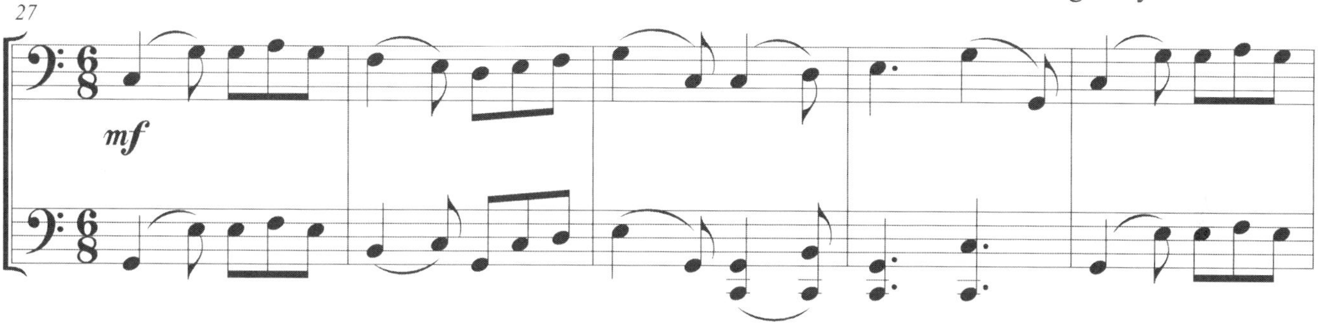

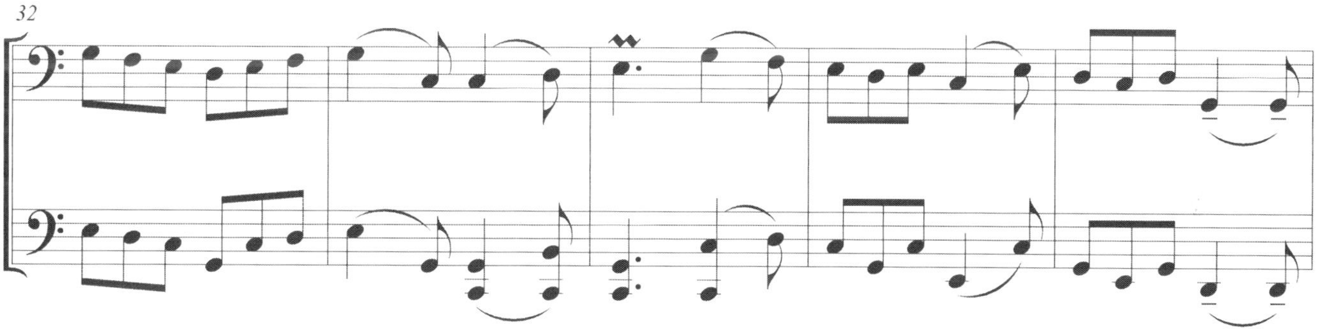

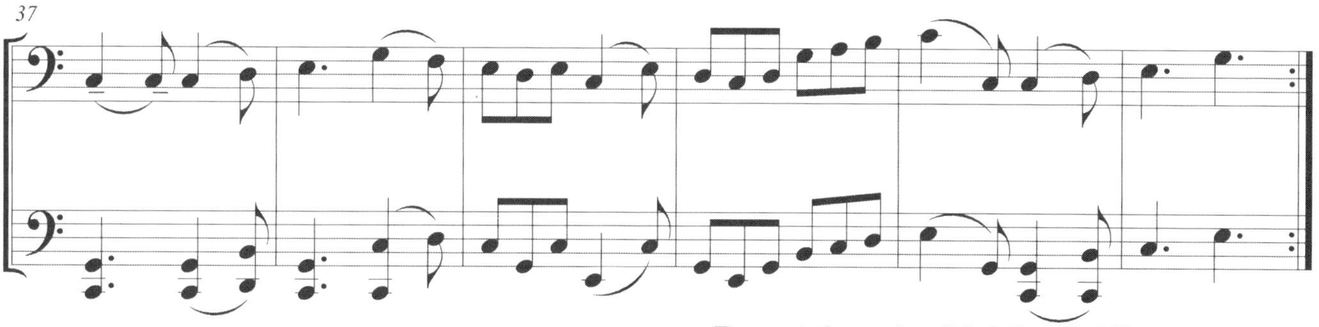

Repeat then play Mairi's Wedding once more.

Cawdor Fair

Arranged by Anne Witt

Loudon's Bonnie Woods

Arranged by Anne Witt

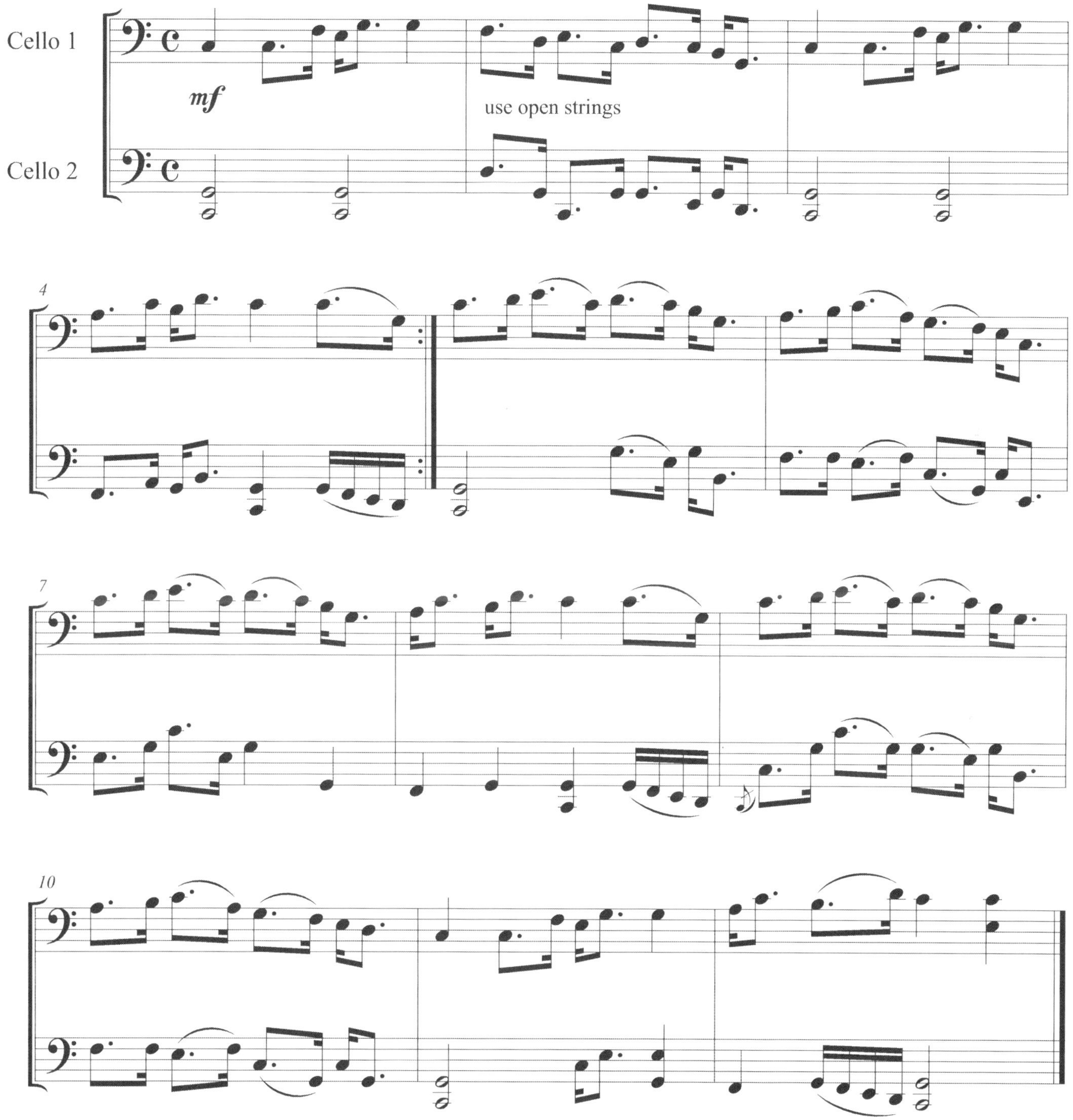

Lochnagar

This is an old air to which Lord Byron (1788-1824) wrote lyrics.

Duncan Davidson

Wha'll be King but Charlie?*

Arranged by Anne Witt

*Wha is Scots dialect for who (pronounced wah) and is referring to Bonnie Prince Charlie.
  Lady Nairne (1766-1845) wrote lyrics to this old tune.

It was all for our Rightful King

Arranged by Anne Witt

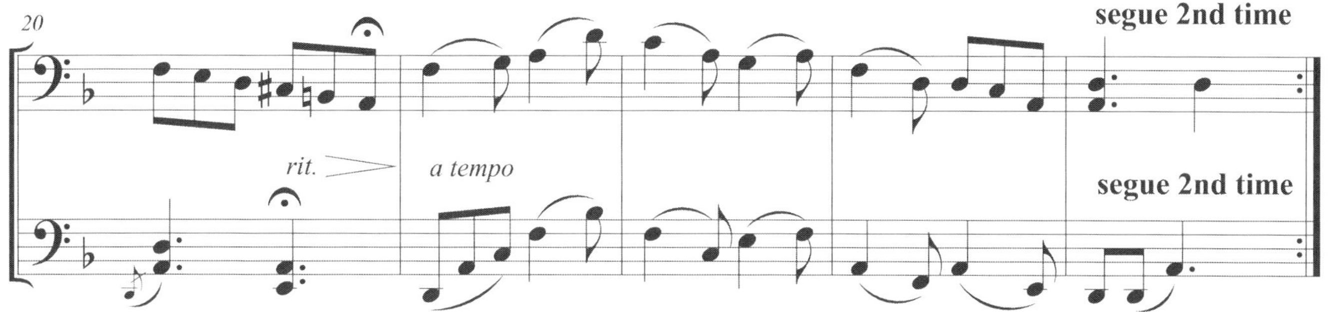

13

Drunk at Night, Dry in the Morning

Arranged by Anne Witt

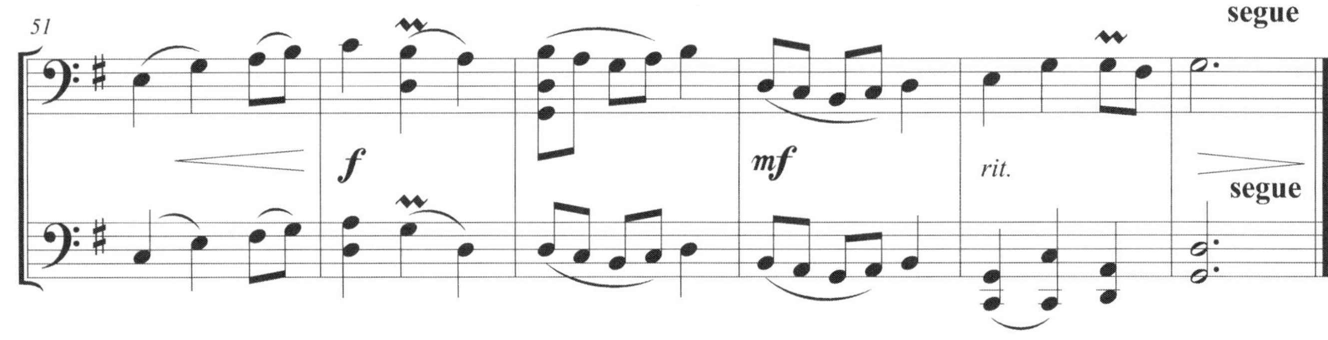

Highland Whisky

Neil Gow (1727-1807)

Arranged by Anne Witt

Haste to the Wedding

Arranged by Anne Witt

John Anderson, My Jo*

Arranged by Anne Witt

Slowly and tenderly ♩ = 76

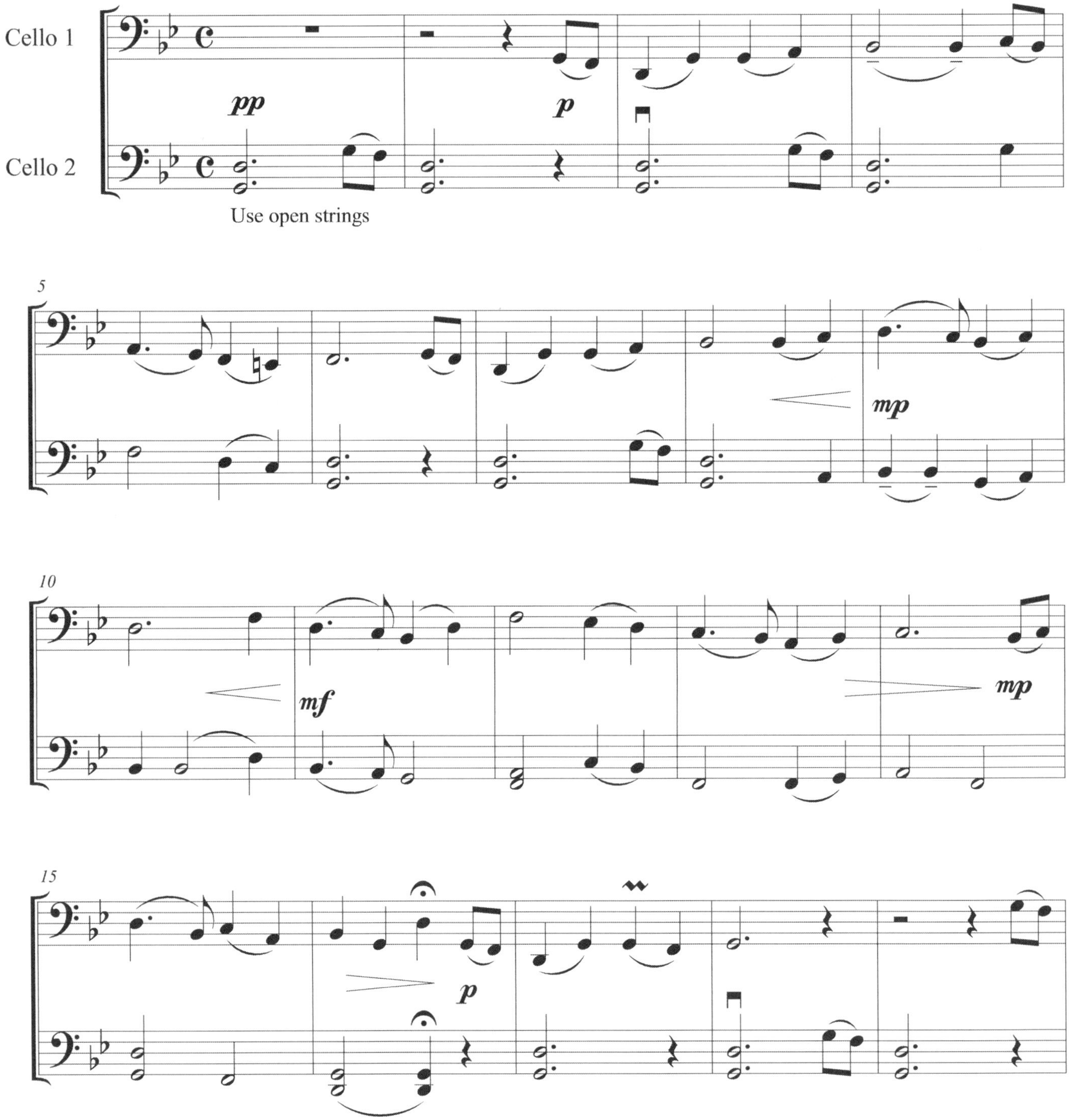

*This is a song by Robert Burns (1759-1796). "Jo" is Scots dialect for "dear."

20
25
mp
mf
29
mp
no vibrato
33
p
pp

Balooloo, My Lammie

Arranged by Anne Witt

This is an old air to which Lady Nairne (1766-1845) wrote lyrics.

20
25
espress.
mf
30
35
p
no vibrato
molto ritard
use open strings

21

Middling, Thank You

Arranged by Anne Witt

Glen Lyon

Arranged by Anne Witt

Over the Seas and Far Awa'

Arranged by Anne Witt

This 18th century air was popular throughout the British Isles and North America. It is also known as "Over the Hills and Far Away." "Away" in Scots dialect is pronounced "a-wah."

Jenny Nettles

Arranged by Anne Witt

Fairest and Dearest

This is an old gaelic air.

Jock o'Hazeldean

Arranged by Anne Witt

This is an old air to which Sir Walter Scott (1771-1832) wrote lyrics.

Major Mole

Arranged by Anne Witt

Glenburnie Rant

Arranged by Anne Witt

Prince Charlie

Repeat Glenburnie Rant, then Prince Charlie.

Prince Charlie is Charles Edward Stuart (1720-1788) or Bonnie Prince Charlie.

Prince Charlie's* Last View of Scotland

Arranged by Anne Witt

*Prince Charlie is Charles Edward Stuart (1720-1788) or Bonnie Prince Charlie.